# ETHICAL HACKING

## MAGIC OF MODERN WORLD!!

CYBERFLASH

# Contents

*Preface* *v*

1. Abbreviations 1

2. Terminologies 4

3. What Is Ethical Hacking ? 8

**Types Of Hacking**

4. Scope In This Sector 13

5. Road Map 15

6. Additional Skills Required 17

7. Network Basics 19

8. Resources 27

Conclusion 31

# PREFACE

This book is designed for those who just wanted to start their career in Ethical Hacking. I am not going to tell you about social media account Hacking. The goal of this book is to teach everyone the basics of hacking and tell you how to start in this field as a beginner. **"Hacking -magic of the modern world"** Makes the world of hacking more accessible by providing you the roadmap of Ethical Hacking. In our second edition, we will discuss how to perform hacking attacks & how to perform penetration tests!

# I

# ABBREVIATIONS

*BY - CYBERFLASH*

To start learning, we should learn about terminologies and abbreviations related to Hacking. Do you feel dumb when you don't know the meaning of a certain term? Well, then this will certainly help you out! If you are ever unsure about anything, simply scroll down and find that specific word, then read the definition. The list is in alphabetical order for convenience!

1. ABBREVIATIONS

- **DDoS** = Distributed Denial of Service
- **Dr. DoS** = Distributed Reflected Denial of Service Attack, uses a list of reflection servers or other methods. such as DNS to spoof an attack to look like it's coming from multiple IPs. Amplification of power in the attack could occur.
- **FTP** = File Transfer Protocol. Used for transferring files over an FTP server.
- **FUD** = Fully Undetectable
- **Hex** = In computer science, hexadecimal refers to base-16 numbers. These are numbers that use digits in the range: 0123456789ABCDEF. In the C programming language (as well as Java, JavaScript, C++, and other places), hexadecimal numbers are prefixed by an Ox. In this manner, one can tell that the

number 0x80 is equivalent to 128 decimal, not 80 decimal.

- **HTTP** = HyperText Transfer Protocol. The foundation of data communication for the World Wide Web.
- **IRC** = Internet Relay Chat. Transmitting text messages in real-time between online users.
- **JDB** = Java drive-by, a very commonly used web-based exploit that allows an attacker to download and execute malicious code locally on a slave's machine through a widely known java vulnerability.
- **Nix** = Unix-based operating system, usually referred to here when referring to DoS'ing.
- **POP3** = This is the most popular protocol for picking up e-mail from a server
- **R. A.T** = Remote Administration Tool
- **SDB** = Silent drive-by, using a zero-day web-based exploit to hiddenly and un-detectably download and execute malicious code on a slave's system. (similar to a JDB however no notification or warning is given to the user)
- **SE**= Social Engineering
- **Skid** = Script Kid/Script Kiddie
- **SMTP** = A TCP/IP protocol used in sending and receiving e-mail.
- **SQL** = Structured Query Language. It's a programming language, that is used to communicate with databases and DBMS. Can go along with a word after it, such as "SQL Injection."
- **SSH** = Secure Shell, used to connect to Virtual Private Servers.
- **TCP** = Transmission Control Protocol, creates connections and exchanges packets of data.
- **UDP** = User Datagram Protocol, An alternative data transport to TCP used for DNS, Voice over IP, and file sharing.
- **VPN** = Virtual Private Network
- **VPS =** Virtual Private Server
- **XSS (CSS)** = Cross Site Scripting
- **TTL** = Time-To-Live
- **WIPS** = Wireless intrusion prevention system
- **NTP** = Network time Protocol

- **PKI** = Public key infrastructure

# II

# TERMINOLOGIES

*BY - CYBERFLASH*

- **Adware**: Adware is software designed to force pre-chosen ads to display on your system.
- Attack: An attack is an action that is done on a system to get its access and extract sensitive data.
- **Back door**: A back door, or trap door, is a hidden entry to a computing device or software that bypasses security measures, such as logins and password protections.
- Bot: A bot is a program that automates an action so that it can be done repeatedly at a much higher rate for a more sustained period than a human operator could do it. For example, sending HTTP, FTP, or Telnet at a higher rate or calling script to create objects at a higher rate.
- **Brute force attack:** A brute force attack is an automated and the simplest kind of method to gain access to a system or website. It tries a different combination of usernames and passwords, over and over again, until it gets in.
- **Buffer Overflow**: Buffer Overflow is a flaw that occurs when more data is written to a block of memory, or buffer, than the buffer, is allocated to hold.

- **Clone phishing:** Clone phishing is the modification of an existing, legitimate email with a false link to trick the recipient into providing personal information.
- **Cracker:** A cracker modifies the software to access the person cracking the software, especially copy protection features.
- **Denial of service attack (DoS):** A denial of service (DoS) attack is a malicious attempt to make a server or a network resource unavailable to users, usually by temporarily interrupting or suspending the services of a host connected to the Internet.
- **Exploit Kit:** An exploit kit is a software system designed to run on web servers, to identify software vulnerabilities in client machines communicating with it, and exploit discovered vulnerabilities to upload and execute malicious code on the client.
- **Exploit:** Exploit is a piece of software, a chunk of data, or a sequence of commands that takes advantage of a bug or vulnerability to compromise the security of a computer or network system.
- **Firewall:** A firewall is a filter designed to keep unwanted intruders outside a computer system or network while allowing safe communication between systems and users on the inside of the firewall.
- **Keystroke logging:** Keystroke logging is the process of tracking the keys which are pressed on a computer (and which touchscreen points are used). It is simply the map of a computer/human interface. It is used by gray and black hat hackers to record login IDs and passwords. Keyloggers are usually secreted onto a device using a Trojan delivered by a phishing email.
- **Logic bomb:** A virus secreted into a system that triggers a malicious action when certain conditions are met. The most common version is the time bomb.
- **Malware:** Malware is an umbrella term used to refer to a variety of forms of hostile or intrusive software, including computer viruses, worms, Trojan horses, ransomware, spyware, adware, scareware, and other malicious programs.

- **Master Program:** A master program is a program a black hat hacker uses to remotely transmit commands to infected zombie drones, normally to carry out Denial of Service attacks or spam attacks.
- **Phishing:** Phishing is an e-mail fraud method in which the perpetrator sends out legitimate-looking emails, in an attempt to gather personal and financial information from recipients.
- **Phreaker:** Phreakers are considered the original computer hackers and they are those who break into the telephone network illegally, typically to make free long-distance phone calls or to tap phone lines.
- **Rootkit:** Rootkit is a stealthy type of software, typically malicious, designed to hide the existence of certain processes or programs from normal methods of detection and enable continued privileged access to a computer.
- **Shrink Wrap code:** A Shrink Wrap code attack is an act of exploiting holes in unpatched or poorly configured software.
- **Social engineering:** Social engineering implies deceiving someone to acquire sensitive and personal information, like credit card details or user names and passwords.
- **Spam:** A Spam is simply an unsolicited email, also known as junk email, sent to a large number of recipients without their consent
- **Spoofing:** Spoofing is a technique used to gain unauthorized access to computers, whereby the intruder sends messages to a computer with an IP address indicating that the message is coming from a trusted host.
- **Spyware:** Spyware is software that aims to gather information about a person or organization without their knowledge and that may send such information to another entity without the consumer's consent, or that asserts control over a computer without the consumer's knowledge.
- **SQL Injection:** SQL injection is an SQL code injection technique, used to attack data-driven applications, in which malicious SQL statements are inserted into an entry field for execution (e.g. to

dump the database contents to the attacker

- **Threat:** A threat is a possible danger that can exploit an existing bug or vulnerability to compromise the security of a computer or network system.
- **Trojan:** A Trojan, or Trojan Horse, is a malicious program disguised to look like a valid program, making it difficult to distinguish from programs that are supposed to be there designed to destroy files, alter information, steal passwords, or other information.
- **Virus:** A virus is a malicious program or a piece of code that is capable of copying itself and typically has a detrimental effect, such as corrupting the system or destroying data.
- **Vulnerability:** A vulnerability is a weakness that allows a hacker to compromise the security of a computer or network system.
- **Worms:** A worm is a self-replicating virus that does not alter files but resides in active memory and duplicates itself.
- **Cross-site Scripting:** Cross-site scripting (XSS) is a type of computer security vulnerability typically found in web applications. XSS enables. attackers to inject client-side script into web pages viewed by other users.
- **Zombie Drone:** A Zombie Drone is defined as a hi-jacked computer that is being used anonymously as a soldier or 'drone' for malicious activity, for example, distributing unwanted spam e-mails.

# III

# WHAT IS ETHICAL HACKING ?

*BY - CYBERFLASH*

Hacking is a futuristic profession but it is surely not easy. To become a hacker one has to have an attitude and curiosity of learning and adapting new skills. You must have a deep knowledge of computer systems, programming languages, operating systems, and the journey of learning goes on and on. Even an Expert Ethical Hacker is still learning.

Hacking has two sides i.e, White Hat Hacking and Black Hat Hacking. The way to differentiate between them is Authorization. Authorization is the process of asking for approval from an Organization or a Company before Conducting any Tests or Attacks. The White Hat is the legal way of Hacking by obtaining approval from an organization while the Black Hat is purely illegal.

We are going to talk about White Hat Hacking in this book.

Hacking is the act of finding the possible entry points that exist in a computer system or a computer network and finally entering into them. Hacking is usually done to gain unauthorized access to a computer system or a computer network, either to harm the systems or to steal sensitive information available on the computer. Hacking is usually legal as long as it is being done to find weaknesses in a computer or network system for testing purposes. This sort of hacking is called Ethical Hacking. A computer expert who does the act of hacking is called a "Hacker" and a person who does hacking to protect or to make the system more secure is known as Ethical Hacker. Ethical hackers know how to find and exploit vulnerabilities and weaknesses in various systems-just like a malicious hacker (or a black hat hacker).

Even they both use the same skills; however, an ethical hacker uses those skills legitimately or lawfully to try to find vulnerabilities and fix them before the bad guys can get there and try to break in. An ethical hacker's role is similar to that of a penetration tester, but it involves broader duties. They break into systems legally and ethically. This is the primary difference between ethical hackers and real hackers - the legality.

**Steps to Perform Ethical Hacking :**

1. **Reconnaissance** refers to the pre-attack phase where an attacker observes a target before launching an attack. It may include the target organization's clients, employees, operations, network, and systems

2. **Scanning** is the phase immediately preceding the attack. Here, the attacker uses the details gathered during reconnaissance to identify specific vulnerabilities. An attacker can gather critical network information such as the mapping of systems, routers, and firewalls by using simple tools such as the standard Windows utility Traceroute.

3. **Gaining Access** In this phase in which real hacking occurs. Attackers use vulnerabilities identified during the reconnaissance and scanning phase to gain access to the target system or network. Attackers gain access to the target system locally, over a LAN, or the Internet.

4.**Maintaining Access** to the target machine and remaining undetected. Attackers install a backdoor or a Trojan to gain repeat access. They can also install rootkits at the kernel level to gain full administrative access to the target computer. Rootkits are used to gain access at the operating system level, while a Trojan horse gains access at the application level. Both rootkits and Trojans require users to install them locally.

5. Clearing Tracks is for avoiding legal trouble, attackers will overwrite the server, System, and application logs to Avoid suspicion and erase all evidence of their actions. Attackers can execute scripts in the Trojan or rootkit to replace the critical system and log files to hide their presence in the system. Terminology

**Elements of Information Security :**

Information Security is a state of well-being of information and infrastructure in which the possibility of theft, tampering, and disruption of information and services is kept low or tolerable.

- Confidentiality
- Authenticity
- Integrity
- Non-Repudiation
- Authorization
- Availability

**"Always Remember Hacking Insta or WiFi won't get you a Job, Penetration Testing and Bug Hunting Will!"**

# Types of Hacking

*BY - CYBERFLASH*

We can segregate hacking into different categories, based on what is being hacked. Here is a set of examples:

- **Website Hacking:** Hacking a website means taking unauthorized control over a web server and its associated software such as databases and other interfaces.

- **Network Hacking:** Hacking a network means gathering information about a network by using tools like Telnet, NS lookup, Ping, Tracert, Netstat, etc. with the intent to harm the network system and hamper its operation.

- **Email Hacking:** It includes getting unauthorized access to an email account and using it without taking the consent of its owner.

- **Ethical Hacking:** Ethical hacking involves finding weaknesses in a computer or network system for testing purposes and finally getting them fixed.

- **Password Hacking:** This is the process of recovering secret passwords from data that has been stored in or transmitted by a computer system.

- **Computer Hacking:** This is the process of stealing computer ID and password by applying hacking methods and getting unauthorized access to a computer system.

- **Virus:** These are discharged by the hacker into the filters of the net website once they enter into it. The purpose is to corrupt the information or resources on the net website.

- **Cracking Password:** Hackers will get your credentials through the style of mean, however, ordinarily, they're doing this through a follow known as key-logging.

- **Malware-Injection Devices:** Cyber-criminals will use hardware to sneak malware onto your pc. you will have detected infected USB sticks which can offer hackers remote access to your device as presently as they are blocked into your pc.

ꝏ

# IV
# SCOPE IN THIS SECTOR

*BY - CYBERFLASH*

Coming years (let's say it as post-COVID-19 pandemic), are very civilized with more digital attacks. As we can say that all the countries are becoming digital, with that more cyber crimes are possible. So the industries required more and more cybersecurity officers with the right skills. As of surveys, there is a need for more than 4 million candidates with the right skills in IT security. So, if you are interested in doing cybersecurity as a career, start adapting the core skills from the basics of networking to getting one's device under your control with proper ethics.

Over recent years, the demand for ethical hackers has been on rising. which gives an assurance of immense job opportunities and higher salary benefits. Some of the World's largest companies like Barclays, JPMorgan Chase, Bank of America, etc. were found in the review of available jobs. This shows that becoming a certified Ethical hacker can open you the doors of career opportunities worldwide.

**Let's know in the Figures.**

Certified ethical hackers make an average annual income of $80,074, according to Payscale. The average starting salary for a certified ethical hacker is $95,000, according to EC Council senior director Steven Graham. The founder of NoWires Security, Eric Geier, estimates a more conservative $50,000 to $100,000 per year in the first years of work depending on your employer, experience, and education. Those with a few years of experience can pull $120,000 and upwards per year, particularly those who work as independent consultants.

# V

# ROAD MAP

*BY - CYBERFLASH*

If you want to make a career in cybersecurity and ethical hacking. Then you have to start with these steps. These steps will help you to drive fast in this field:

1. First and most important you should have a mindset of 'Never Give Up'. You should have to try again and again.

2. You'll have to learn most of the terminologies & basics of Software and Hardware.

3. Now, you'll have to learn Linux (any Distro). I prefer Kali Linux. This Distro is used by almost all of the Penetration Tester and Hacker. While you have many other options such as parrot os, Ubuntu, etc.

4. One of the most important skills to become an ethical hacker is networking skills. The computer network is nothing but the interconnection of multiple devices, generally termed as Hosts connected using multiple paths to send/receive data or media. Understanding networks like DHCP, Supernetting, Subnetting, network protocols, and more will provide ethical hackers to explore the various interconnected computers in a network and the potential security threats that this might create, as well as how to handle those threats. To Learn computer networking refer CCNA course. You can learn it from any online platform like youtube,

udemy, etc.

5. Another most important skill to become an ethical hacker is Programming Skills. Learn at least one client and server-side programming language. I recommend Python to start with. As it is easy or you can choose any other language. Some of the Coding languages you should learn: C Language, Python, Ruby, Bash Scripting, HTML, Javascript, SQL, PHP, etc

6. Learn how to do Scanning, information gathering, and enumerating.

7. Learn about Server-side and client-side hacking attacks and how to perform those attacks.

8. Now, Get your hands dirty with popular backing tools like Nmap, Metasploit, john the Ripper, etc.

9. Now that you have a solid starting point in your career, your next focus is to master your skills and continue to learn. Doing the research, in the beginning, exposes you to the fact that the technology field is ever-changing and you will be constantly learning to keep up with the industry. To become an expert, you must be willing to continuously evolve and be self-taught in most cases. Most senior positions would prefer some sort of formal education but it is not required. To combat this, acquiring certifications is a must.

**Several certifications will prove your skill and knowledge for Ethical Hacking:**

- SANS GIAC certification
- Certified Vulnerability Assessor
- Certified Professional Ethical Hacker(CPEN)
- Certified Penetration Testing Engineer (CPTE)
- Certified Ethical Hacker (CEH)
- Offensive Security Certified Professional (OSCP)
- CompTIA Security +

# VI

# Additional Skills required

*BY - CYBERFLASH*

**A. Reverse Engineering -**

Reverse Engineering is a process of recovering the design, requirement specifications, and functions of a product from an analysis of its code. It builds a program database and generates information from this. The objective of reverse engineering is to expedite the maintenance work by improving the understandability of a system and to produce the necessary documents for a legacy system. In software security, reverse engineering is widely used to ensure that the system lacks any major security flaws or vulnerabilities. It helps to make a system robust, thereby protecting it from hackers and spyware. You can learn Assembly Language for reverse engineering.

**B. Cryptography -**

Cryptography is the study and application of techniques for reliable communication in the presence of third parties called adversaries. It deals with developing and analyzing protocols that prevent malicious third parties from retrieving information being shared between two entities thereby following the various aspects of information security. Cryptography deals with converting a normal text/message known as plain text to a non-readable form known as ciphertext during the transmission to make it incomprehensible to hackers.

**C. Database Skills -**

DBMS is the crux of creating and managing all databases. Accessing a database where all the information is stored can put the company in a tremendous threat, so ensuring that this software is hack-proof is important. An ethical hacker must-have. a good understanding of this, along with different database engines and data schemas to help the organization build a strong DBMS.

**D. Problem Solving Skills -**

Problem-solving skills help one to determine the source of a problem and find an effective solution. Apart from the technical skills pointed above, an ethical hacker also must be a critical thinker and dynamic problem solver. They must be wanting to learn new ways and ensure all security breaches are thoroughly checked. This requires tons. of testing and an ingenious penchant to devise new ways of problem-solving.

# VII

# NETWORK BASICS

A network is a group of two or more computer systems or other devices that are linked together to exchange data. In networks, computing devices exchange data with each other using data links between nodes. These data links are established with the help of cable media such as wires or wireless media such as WiFi.

**Network Components and Functions**

**Server:** A computer or device on a network that manages network resources. Servers are often dedicated, meaning that they perform no other tasks besides their server tasks like accepting and responding to requests made by another program, known as a client.

**Client:** A client is an application that runs on a personal computer or workstation and relies on a server to perform some operations. The client accesses the server by way of a network.

**Devices:** Computer devices, such as a CD-ROM drive or printer, that are not part of the essential computer. Examples of devices include disk drives, printers, and modems.

**Hub:** Hub is a network hardware device for connecting multiple devices and making them act as a single network segment. A hub works at the physical layer of the OSI model.

**Switch:** A device that filters and forwards packets between LAN segments. Switches operate at the data link layer and sometimes the network layer of the OSI Reference Model.

**Router:** A router is a device that is capable of forwarding data packets to a network. Routers are placed at the junction (gateway) of two or more networks connect. Routers use headers and forwarding tables to determine the best path for forwarding the packets.

**Bridge:** Bridge is a computer networking device that connects a local area network (LAN) to another local area network that uses the same protocol.

**Access Point:** A hardware device or a computer's software that acts as a communication hub for users to connect all their wireless devices.

**Types of Networks:**

**Local area network (LAN):**

A LAN is a network that connects computers and devices in a limited geographical area such as a home, school, office building.

**Wide area network (WAN):** A WAN is a computer network that covers a large geographic area such as a city, country, or spans even intercontinental distances. A WAN uses a communications channel that combines many types of media such as telephone lines, ethernet cables, optical fibers, etc

**Metropolitan Area Networks (MAN):** Metropolitan area Network covers a larger area than that of a LAN and smaller area when compared to WAN. MANs rarely extend beyond 100 KM and comprise a combination of different hardware and transmission media.

**Wireless Local Area Network (WLAN):** Wireless local area networks provide wireless network communication over short distances using radio or infrared signals instead of traditional network cabling. WLANs are built by attaching a device called the access point to the edge of the wired network. Clients communicate with the AP using a wireless network adapter similar in function to a traditional Ethernet adapter.

**Virtual private network (VPN):** The virtual private network is an overlay network in which some of the links between nodes are carried by virtual circuits in the network instead of physical wires.

The data link layer protocols of the virtual network are said to be tunneled through the network.

**Personal Area Network (PAN):** A personal area network is a computer network organized around an individual. Personal area networks typically involve mobile devices. Personal area networks can be wired or wirelessly. These networks generally cover a network range of 10 meters (about 30 feet).

**OSI model:**

OSI (Open Systems Interconnection) is a reference model for how applications communicate over a network. The main concept of OSI is that the process of communication between two endpoints in a network can be divided into seven distinct groups of related functions or layers. Each communicating user or program is on a device that can provide those seven layers of function. The seven Open Systems Interconnection layers are:

**Layer 1:**

**Physical Layer:** This layer conveys the bit stream across the network either electrically, mechanically, or through radio waves. The physical layer covers a variety of devices and mediums, among them cabling, connectors, receivers, transceivers, and repeaters.

**Layer 2:**

**Data Link Layer:** This layer sets up links across the physical network, putting packets into network frames. This layer has two sublayers the logical link control layer and the media access control layer (MAC). MAC layer types include Ethernet and 802.11 wireless specifications.

**Layer 3:**

**Network Layer:** This layer handles addressing and routing the data. To transfer it from the right source to the right destination. The IP address is part of the network layer.

**Layer 4:**

**Transport Layer:** This layer manages packetization of data, then the delivery of the packets, including checking for errors in the data once it arrives. On the internet, TCP and UDP provide these services for most applications.

**Layer 5:**

**Session Layer:** The session layer controls the connections between computers. It establishes, manages, and terminates the connections between the local and remote applications.

**Layer 6:**

**Presentation Layer:** This layer is usually part of an operating system (OS) and converts incoming and outgoing data from one presentation format to another for example, from clear text to encrypted text at one end and back to clear text at the other.

**Layer 7:**

**Application Layer:** The application layer of the OSI model interacts with the end-user. Protocols at this layer handle the requests from different software applications. If a web browser wants to download an image, an email client wants to check the server, and a file-sharing program wants to upload a movie, the protocols in the application layer will process those requests.

##short form to remember -**APSTNDP ###**

IP address An Internet Protocol address (IP address) is a numerical label assigned to each device connected to a computer network. An IP address serves two purposes, host or network interface identification and location addressing. Internet Protocol version 4 (IPv4) defines an IP address as a 32-bit number and a new version of IP (IPv6), uses 128 bits for the IP address.

**Private IP address:** A private IP address is a non-Internet facing IP address. Private IP addresses are provided by network devices, such as routers, using network address translation (NAT)

**Public IP address:** A public IP address is an IP address that can be accessed over the Internet. The public IP address is a globally unique IP address assigned to a computing device.

**IPv4:** Internet Protocol Version 4 is the fourth revision of the Internet Protocol used to identify devices on a network. IPv4 is the most widely deployed Internet protocol used to connect devices to the Internet. IPv4 uses a 32-bit address scheme allowing a total of 2^32 addresses.

**IPv6:** Internet Protocol Version 6 is the newest version of the Internet Protocol reviewed in the IETF standards committees to replace the current version of IPv4. IPv6 addresses are 128-bit IP addresses written in hexadecimal and separated by colons. An example IPv6 address could be written like this 3ffe: 1900:4545:3:200: f8ff: fe21:67cf.

**IP address classes**: There are five classes of IP addresses, they are Class A, Class B, Class C, Class D, and Class E, where only A, B, and C are commonly used.

**Class: Address Range : Supports:**

- Class A 1.0.0.1 to 126.255.255.254 Supports 16 million hosts on each of 127 networks.
- Class B 128.1.0.1 to 191.255.255.254 Supports 65,000 hosts on each of 16,000 networks.
- Class C 192.0.1.1 to 223.255.254.254 Supports 254 hosts on each of 2 million networks.
- Class D 224.0.0.0 to 239.255.255.255 Reserved for multicast groups.
- Class E 240.0.0.0 to 254.255.255.254 Reserved for future use, or Research and Development Purposes.

**Subnetwork (Subnet):**

A subnet is a logical subdivision of an IP network. Dividing a network into two or more networks is known as subnetting. Computers that belong to a subnet are addressed with a significant bit-group in their IP addresses. Subnetting results in the logical division of an IP address into two parts, the network address, and the host identifier.

**Super network (Supernet):**

Supernet is an Internet Protocol network that is formed, for combining two or more networks into a larger network. The benefits of supernetting are conservation of address space, gaining efficiency regarding memory storage, and route information processing.

**Network address translation:**

Network address translation (NAT) is a method of remapping one IP address space into another by modifying network address information in IP header packets while they are in transit. It has become a popular and essential tool in conserving global address space in the face of IPv4 address exhaustion.

**Dynamic Host Configuration Protocol:**

The Dynamic Host Configuration Protocol (DHCP) is a network management protocol used on UDP/IP networks. A DHCP server dynamically assigns an IP address and other network configuration parameters to each device on a network so that it can communicate with other IP networks.

**TCP:**

TCP stands for Transmission Control Protocol, which is a widely used protocol for data transmission over a network. TCP establishes a connection between two hosts before transmitting data, to ensure that data transmitted over the network reaches the destination without fail. TCP also known as a connection-oriented protocol, establishes a reliable connection between sender and receiver. TCP provides error and flow control mechanisms that help in the orderly transmission of data and retransmission of lost packets.

**UDP:**

UDP stands for User Datagram Protocol, which is a connectionless protocol, mostly used for connections that can tolerate data loss. UDP is used by applications on the internet that offer voice and video communications, which can suffer some data loss without adversely affecting the quality. UDP does not provide error and flow control mechanisms because of which it does not require a connection to be established before transmitting data over the network.

**ICMP**:

ICMP stands for Internet Control Message Protocol; this is widely used for internet communication troubleshooting or generated in response to errors in IP operations, this will send packets to the target machine and will see whether the packets are delivered or not.

**Address Resolution Protocol:**

Address Resolution Protocol (ARP) is a communication protocol used for discovering the link-layer address, such as a MAC address, associated with a given network layer address. This mapping is a critical function in the Internet Protocol Suite. It works within the boundaries of a single network never routed across internetworking nodes. ARP uses a simple message format containing one address resolution request or response. The size of the ARP message depends on the link layer and network layer address sizes.

**Domain Name System :**

Domain Name System (DNS) is a naming system for resources connected to the Internet or a private network. The DNS is responsible for assigning domain names and mapping those names to Internet resources by designating name servers for each domain. Network administrators have authority over the subdomains of their allocated namespace to other name servers. Domain Name System is an essential component of Internet functionality.

**Internet Group Management Protocol:**

Internet Group Management Protocol (IGMP) is a communication protocol used by hosts and adjacent routers on IPv4 networks to establish multicast group memberships. IGMP is an integral part of IP multicast. IGMP can be used for one-to-many networking applications such as online video streaming and gaming and allows the more efficient use of resources.

**Routing:**

Routing is the process of selecting a path for traffic in a network or across multiple networks. In routing, network packets from their source toward their destination are routed through intermediate network nodes by specific packet forwarding mechanisms. Intermediate nodes are typically networked hardware devices such as routers, bridges, gateways, firewalls, or switches. In routing, process packets are directed based on routing tables, which maintain a record of the routes to various network destinations. An administrator specifies the routing table.

**Routing protocol:**

A routing protocol specifies how routers communicate with each other, distributing information, which enables them to select routes between any two nodes on a computer network. Routing algorithms determine to choose a specific route. A routing protocol shares this information first among immediate neighbors, and then throughout the network. The major types of routing protocols.

- Routing Information Protocols (RIP)
- Interior Gateway Routing Protocol (IGRP)
- Open Shortest Path First (OSPF)
- Exterior Gateway Protocol (EGP)
- Enhanced Interior Gateway Routing Protocol (EIGRP)
- Border Gateway Protocol (BGP)
- Intermediate System-to-Intermediate System (IS-IS)

# VIII

# Resources

*BY - CYBERFLASH*

**A. To Learn Linux Online Platforms from where you can start your learning about Linux:**

**Websites:**

- compute freely.org
- linuxnewbieguide.org
- makeuseof.com

**Youtube Channels:**

- · LearnLinuxTV
- thenewboston

**B. For Computer Networking:**

Some of the best platforms from where you can Computer Networking in a very convenient manner:

**Websites:**

- study-ccna.com - https://study-ccna.com
- ciscopress.com -https://www.ciscopress.com

**Youtube Channels:**

- CCNA Free Cisco Training -"Networking"
- Computer Networks Course -Ravindrababu Ravula
- Computer Networking Tutorials -thenewboston

**C. For Programming Languages**

Some of the best platforms from where you can learn how to code:

**Websites:**

- freeCodeCamp
- Codecademy
- Coursera
- SoloLearn
- W3Schools

**Youtube Channels:**

- thenewboston
- Programming with Mosh

**D. To Learn about Hacking**

Some of the platforms from where you can learn about Hacking Attacks and how to perform them:

**Websites:**

- cybrary.it
- security tube
- udemy
- simplilearn.com
- Edureka
- sectools.org
- Hackaday

**Youtube Channels:**

- Hackersploit
- Cyber Mentor
- Bitten Tech

**E. Essential Websites to Practise your Hacking Skills:**

As you all know, practice is necessary for this field. We use some of the Sites which provide vulnerable machines, challenges, STC for practicing our Hacking Skills.

- Hack the Box
- Hack this Site
- testphp.vulnweb.com
- Over the Wire
- OWASP Juice Shop Project
- Root-me.org

You can also install a Vulnerable machine on your Localhost:

- DWV
- Mutillidae
- DIVA

**We can also play CTFs to boost up our hacking skills.**

CTF (Capture The Flag) is a kind of information security competition that challenges contestants to solve a variety of tasks ranging from a scavenger hunt on Wikipedia to basic programming exercises to hacking your way into a server to steal data. In these challenges, the contestant is usually asked to find a specific piece of text that may be hidden on the server or behind a webpage. This goal is called the flag, hence the name!

- ctfs.github.io/resources
- ctftime.org/writeups
- trailofbits.github.io/ctf/forensics/es
- picoctf,com
- hackthebox.eu
- ctftime.org

**F. Some Extra Points:**

Read some Hacking Books because it

will teach you a lot more stuff. If you are fond of watching movies,

do watch hacking movies.

Choose your Mentor because he will solve your problems and motivate you to cross all the Hurdles.

# Conclusion

**As I said earlier this book is only for those who are thinking to start their career in Ethical Hacking and want a simplified guide. In our Books, we will talk about how to perform attacks, how to use hacking tools & how to earn from Penetration Testing. We will also talk about Hacking with Android.**

**REFER MEDIUM ACCOUNT @ CYBERFLASH**

**THANK YOU!!**

**BY - CYBERFLASH**

ꕤ

9 798886 298345

Printed by Libri Plureos GmbH in Hamburg,
Germany